SEE HIS GLORY

DAILY READINGS FOR ADVENT

2018 Edition

Mathew Bartlett

See His Glory by Mathew Bartlett

First Published in Great Britain in 2018.

FAITHBUILDERS

An Imprint of Apostolos Publishing Ltd,

3rd Floor, 207 Regent Street,

London W1B 3HH

www.apostolos-publishing.com

British Library Cataloguing-in-Publication Data. A catalogue record for this book is available from the British Library

ISBN: 978-1-912120-75-8

Cover Design by Faithbuilders, London. Cover Images © Adyna | istockphoto.com

Printed and bound in Great Britain by
Marston Book Services Ltd, Oxfordshire

Week One: God Reveals His Glory

Sunday 2nd December: *The Glory of God's Holiness*

> *And in the morning you will see the glory of the Lord, because he has heard your grumbling against him. Who are we, that you should grumble against us? (Exodus 16:7)*

Our goal this advent season will be to tune our hearts to praise God's glory—yet our series of readings begins with a minor, not a major chord. God had promised to reveal his glory to the people of Israel, but regrettably, this was because their unbelief had led to complaining. This angered the Lord, and so God's glory would be revealed to Israel in a demonstration of his holiness and strong opposition against sin.

Yet even in this situation, and even under the "old" covenant, a justifiably angry God still acted in grace toward his people. They had complained about their hunger, and in reply God sent them manna to eat. This miraculous provision of food eradicated hunger and continued every day until Israel entered the promised land.

In Scripture, God's glory is always linked with his grace:

> *The Word became flesh and made his dwelling among us. We have seen his glory, the glory of the one and only Son, who came from the Father, full of grace and truth. (John 1:14).*

Eventually, as the murmuring against God continued, the instigators were severely punished (see Numbers 11). Even so, Israel came to learn that God is "the compassionate and gracious God, slow to anger, abounding in love and faithfulness" (Exodus 34:6). An appreciation of God's glory begins as we realise his goodness in response to our sin.

> **Prayer:** Lord, on this first day of Advent, we thank you that despite our sinfulness and tendency to find fault with you, you have been gracious to us. Every day we experience your extravagant love and generous provision. We celebrate how your glory has been revealed in your Son Jesus. In his name. Amen.

Advent Reading Plan Day One: John 1; Mark 1:1–4.

Monday 3rd December: *The Glory of Worship*

> *Then Moses said, "This is what the Lord has commanded you to do, so that the glory of the Lord may appear to you." ... Moses and Aaron then went into the tent of meeting. When they came out, they blessed the people; and the glory of the Lord appeared to all the people. (Leviticus 9:6, 23)*

Yesterday we discovered how God graciously provided food for his people, despite their sinful complaining. In today's verses, God provides the same people with a way to worship him and see his glory.

How could such a sinful people approach God? The way was made through sacrifice—Leviticus 9 explains how sin offerings were made. The blood of the sin offering is highlighted first (vv. 2–3), for it is the blood which makes atonement for the soul (cf. Leviticus 17:11). These offerings were entirely burned, to indicate their complete dedication to God (vv. 10–11). The offerings were made for both priests and people.

As God's people today, we are no less sinful than God's people of long ago. The New Testament writers see all the sacrifices of the Old Testament as pictures which foreshadow Jesus—the shedding of his precious blood has made atonement for our souls (Romans 3:25), and now we have peace with God (Romans 5:1). Christ offered his life in complete dedication to God (as a burnt offering, see Hebrews 13:11–12).

When Aaron had finished offering all the sacrifices, God revealed his glory to the people (vv. 22–24). When Jesus offered his life as a sacrifice for sin, he was raised to life by the glory of the Father and is now a living expression of God's glory to all people in every age.

> **Prayer:** Lord, thank you that not only at Advent, but always, you reveal your glory to us in the person of your Son. His sacrifice has made the way for us to approach you in worship, that you might reveal your glory in our lives. We praise you in Jesus' name. Amen.

Advent Reading Plan Day Two: John 2; Luke 1:1–4.

Tuesday 4th December: *The Glory of Forgiveness*

> *But the whole assembly talked about stoning them. Then the glory of the Lord appeared at the tent of meeting to all the Israelites. … The Lord replied, "I have forgiven them, as you asked. Nevertheless, as surely as I live and as surely as the glory of the Lord fills the whole earth … not one of them will ever see the land I promised on oath to their ancestors. (Numbers 14:10, 20–23)*

Numbers 14 recounts the well-known story of how the children of Israel rejected the faithful witness of Joshua and Caleb, and so refused to enter the promised land. The people were discussing stoning Joshua and Caleb, when God intervened. The sudden appearance of his glory showed his displeasure. God declared that he was ready to disown his people and build a new dynasty through Moses. Yet Moses stood between God and the people, making intercession for them. God listened and forgave the sin of the people. The rebels would still not enter Canaan, but God would not completely abandon the nation. The people's act of disobedience resulted in their wandering through the desert for 40 years, until every offender had died. Then God promised to take their children into the promised land.

As Christians, we appreciate how Jesus fulfils for us the role which Moses took for his people—that of intercessor. Jesus stands between us and God, as if to remind God of his wounds, and pray for our ongoing forgiveness. "My dear children, I write this to you so that you will not sin. But if anybody does sin, we have an advocate with the Father—Jesus Christ, the Righteous One." (1 John 2:1) Through Jesus, God reveals his glory in our forgiveness.

> **Prayer:** Lord, we confess the times when we have sinned against you. As we humbly ask your forgiveness, we praise you that your mercy and grace to us are sure, for you have given us your Son as one who ever lives to make intercession for us. In Jesus' name. Amen.

Advent Reading Plan Day Three: John 3; Luke 1:5–25.

Wednesday 5th December: *The Glory God's Choice*

> *When Korah had gathered all his followers in opposition to them at the entrance to the tent of meeting, the glory of the Lord appeared to the entire assembly. The Lord said to Moses and Aaron "Separate yourselves from this assembly so I can put an end to them at once." (Numbers 16:19–21)*

It has been a recurring theme of our Old Testament readings this week that the glory of God appears to oppose evil, and to judge or forgive sin. It shows God to be always on the side of right. Korah and his followers opposed God, and in particular his choice of Moses and Aaron to lead the people. As God's glory appears, the Lord warns Moses and Aaron to move away so that he might destroy all the people.

Once again, Moses reveals the hidden purpose in God's heart by interceding for Israel, appealing to God's sense of mercy and justice. As a result, only the guilty parties and their families are judged. Even so, this case, as countless others in the Old Testament, is meant to stand in direct contrast with events in the New Testament.

The people of Moses' day considered it an awesome sight when God brought judgment upon sinners, and the ground opened to swallow Korah alive—revealing Moses to be God's choice as leader. How much more should we be amazed at the manifestation of God's glory in the coming of Christ, which brings kindness to the underserving, love to the unlovable, and forgiveness to sinners! Of Jesus, God says "this is my beloved Son, in whom I am well pleased." Without Christ, we too could expect to receive judgment for our sins. But Christ is God's chosen One, to brings us hope and eternal life.

> **Prayer:** We thank you God for your beloved Son Jesus, who came into this world to be our Saviour. We praise you that he reveals to us, not the glory of your judgment, but the greater glory of your love and kindness. Amen.

Advent Reading Plan Day Four: John 4; Luke 1:26–38.

Thursday 6th December: *God is the Glory of His People*

He who is the Glory of Israel does not lie or change his mind; for he is not a human being, that he should change his mind. (1 Samuel 15:29)

In today's verse, and elsewhere in the Bible, God is described as "the Glory" of his people. What we have in view here is not the glory of God but rather the God of glory!

Whatever God was to his people in the Old Testament, he is all this and much more to his people in the New. These words of 1 Samuel 15:28–29 were spoken to King Saul, concerning the judgment God had pronounced against him. Saul had disobeyed God's clear instructions in time of war, and so his kingship would be taken from him. This pronouncement could not be changed, for God neither lies nor changes his mind.

For the New Testament believer, the words which sounded so threatening to Saul are transformed by Christ's grace into a glorious promise. Through his Son, God gives eternal life to all who believe. He promises that:

Whoever believes in the Son has eternal life. (John 3:36)

Can God lie? Can he change his mind? No! Little wonder, then, that Paul says we can "be greatly encouraged" because of "it is impossible for God to lie" (Hebrews 6:18), and that it was God "who does not lie" who promised us eternal life before time began (Titus 1:2).

As Christians, our glory and boasting are not in ourselves, but in God, who "saved us and called us to a holy life—not because of anything we have done but because of his own purpose and grace." (2 Timothy 1:9)

Prayer: Lord, we take strong comfort from your unchanging purpose, and your irrevocable word of promise, that everlasting life belongs to all who believe in Jesus Christ your Son. In Jesus' name. Amen.

Advent Reading Plan Day Five: John 5; Luke 1:39–56.

Friday 7th December: *Grace and Glory*

> *For the Lord God is a sun and shield; The Lord will give grace and glory; No good thing will He withhold From those who walk uprightly. (Psalm 84:11 NKJV)*

When we first come to God, we are dead in trespasses and sins, but God in receives us by his grace, and through faith in Christ, brings us from spiritual death to spiritual life (Ephesians 2:1–5). He has rescued from sin's power and penalty, having forgiven us all trespasses. In Christ, we are sitting in heavenly places (Ephesians 2:6), since all those who have experienced God's grace are also destined to participate in his glory (Romans 8:30).

One day, we will be "like him, for we shall see him as he is" (1 John 3:2). In his high priestly prayer before his crucifixion, Jesus said:

> *Father, I want those you have given me to be with me where I am, and to see my glory, the glory you have given me because you loved me before the creation of the world. (John 17:24)*

What a wonderful future awaits us!

And yet God's promise of grace and glory does not only embrace life after death. It includes the idea of abundant life before death. *No good thing will He withhold from those who walk uprightly.* God gives us our daily bread. The needs we have every day will be met by the one who feeds the sparrow and clothes the lilies of the field. Plus, we have the blessings of peace with God, fruitful service, a holy life, and love for others, which are all freely given by grace—nothing withheld *from those who walk uprightly.*

> **Prayer:** Lord, we thank you that in Christ you have blessed us with every spiritual blessing, and that you also provide our every earthly blessing. We praise you that by your grace, we shall share in Christ's glory forevermore. Amen.

Advent Reading Plan Day Six: John 6; Luke 1:57–66.

Saturday 8th December: *Declaring God's Glory*

> *Declare his glory among the nations, his marvelous deeds among all peoples. For great is the Lord and most worthy of praise; he is to be feared above all gods. (1 Chronicles 16:24–25)*

As Christians, we have received every blessing from God as a result of his glory being revealed in Jesus Christ. God has done marvellous things for us, and so we must declare his glory to other people in every nation.

No one is ever blessed merely so that they might keep that blessing to themselves. We are blessed for the good of all people. If we have a testimony of what God has done for us—his marvellous, glorious, or praiseworthy deeds—we should be eager to share it with others, that they might in turn become recipients of his goodness.

God's glory is an expression of himself, it is the sum of who he is plus what he has done. To young and old in every nation, let us be sure to make known the glory of our God.

We remember at this season all who are sharing Christ through Christmas carol services, school assemblies, and ministries to the hungry or homeless. Those who visit the isolated or housebound in their own communities, or who travel overseas bringing practical, medical, or spiritual help to those affected by natural or man-made disasters. In these diverse ministries and countless others, the theme of all our service remains the same: we declare the glory of God.

> **Prayer:** Lord, you were born in Bethlehem, in poverty and humility, that you might restore all people to a relationship with God your Father and grant us eternal glory. As you have revealed the glory of your Father to us, help us your servants to declare your glory among all nations. In Jesus' name. Amen.

Advent Reading Plan Day Seven: John 7; Luke 1:67–80.

Week 2: The Prophets Foretell Future Glory

Sunday 9th December: *God's Glory will be Revealed*

And the glory of the Lord will be revealed, and all people will see it together. For the mouth of the Lord has spoken. (Isaiah 40:5)

The prophet Isaiah announced this message to his people as they faced the dark experience of exile, promising a glorious future when not only would they return to their homeland (where God was thought to dwell), but the whole earth would witness the glory of God.

Saint Luke takes hold of this ancient promise and applies it to Jesus. During the ministry of John the Baptist, the first part of Isaiah's prophecy is fulfilled (Isa 40:3–5; Luke 3:4–5). Then in Luke 3:6, the evangelist links this promise with Isaiah 52:10, "The Lord will lay bare his holy arm in the sight of all the nations, and all the ends of the earth will see the salvation of our God." Nothing could reveal God's glory more than his work of salvation in Christ. Jesus brings the knowledge of God not only to his people Israel, but to the whole world. Ultimately, Isaiah promised that "the earth will be filled with the knowledge of the Lord as the waters cover the sea." (Isaiah 11:9)

I am writing this at a time when news reports of fighting in the holy land are common. The fight is over land. But all the earth is God's, and there is room enough for all people to live in peace. If only they would lift up their eyes to see God's salvation, allow unrighteousness to be banished, and acknowledge the glory of God in the face of Jesus Christ. Oh that the days of which Isaiah spoke may come at last!

> **Prayer:** Lord, we thank you for the example of your Son Jesus, the Prince of peace, who makes peace between men and nations. Through him we anticipate the fulfilment of your promise that all flesh will see your salvation, and that this will result in peace, when "the earth shall be filled with the knowledge of the glory of God as the waters cover the sea." In Jesus' name. Amen.

Advent Reading Plan Day Eight: John 8; Luke 2:1–7.

Monday 10th December: *The Glory of the New Covenant*

> *"The days are coming," declares the Lord, "when I will make a new covenant with the people of Israel and with the people of Judah." (Jeremiah 31:31)*

Jesus has come to bring us a greater revelation of God, a closer fellowship with him as Father, and an eternal life with him that was not possible under the old covenant. As we prepare ourselves to celebrate Christ's birth, we consider how Christ's glory surpasses all that has gone before.

The prophet Jeremiah spoke of a "new covenant" replacing the old. No one replaces something good with something inferior, but with something better. Many years later, Jesus announced that this new covenant would be "in my blood" (Luke 22:20), which the writer to the Hebrews refers to as, "the blood of the eternal covenant." Similarly, Paul highlights how the glory of the new covenant is far superior to the old.

> *Now if the ministry that brought death, which was engraved in letters on stone, came with glory, so that the Israelites could not look steadily at the face of Moses because of its glory, transitory though it was, will not the ministry of the Spirit be even more glorious? If the ministry that brought condemnation was glorious, how much more glorious is the ministry that brings righteousness! For what was glorious has no glory now in comparison with the surpassing glory. And if what was transitory came with glory, how much greater is the glory of that which lasts! (2 Corinthians 3:7–11)*

The glory of the new covenant is greater than the old, because Jesus is the perfect expression of the glory of God!

Prayer: Lord, you are the God of all glory. Your glory never changes or diminishes. Yet we praise you that the revelation of your glory given in Jesus surpasses all that has gone before and can never be equalled. In Jesus' name. Amen.

Advent Reading Plan Day Nine: John 9; Luke 2:8–20.

Tuesday 11th December: *Arise, Shine, Forever!*

Arise, shine, for your light has come, and the glory of the Lord rises upon you. See, darkness covers the earth and thick darkness is over the peoples, but the Lord rises upon you and his glory appears over you. (Isaiah 60:1–2)

The prophet Isaiah speaks of a future day of restoration. Christians understand the ultimate fulfilment of this restoration to be in Christ. Since Christ our light has come, we are no longer in darkness. The thick darkness which covers all peoples is a reference to their ignorance of God and his glory. But since, in Christ, this glory has been revealed, there is no reason for them to remain in darkness. Christ has revealed his glory TO US and IN US so that it might be revealed THROUGH US to others. We are to shine as his witnesses in every dark place.

One by one, as men and women put their faith in Christ, they are translated from darkness to light (1 Peter 2:9). Eventually, the completed church will stand before her Lord to see his glory. In heaven:

The sun will no more be your light by day, nor will the brightness of the moon shine on you, for the Lord will be your everlasting light, and your God will be your glory. (Isaiah 60:19)

This advent, we pause to reflect on the future which unites us in Christ, the basis of our hope. Then we go forward to bring the light of the glory of the gospel of Christ, who is the image of God, to others—whoever we meet, whenever we have opportunity.

Prayer: Lord, help us to shine your light into this dark world, that we might offer hope to all those who lack the hope they need for the present and for eternity. In Jesus' name. Amen.

Advent Reading Plan Day Ten: John 10; Luke 2:21–35.

Wednesday 12th December: *Others Drawn to the Glory of God*

And I, because of what they have planned and done, am about to come and gather the people of all nations and languages, and they will come and see my glory. (Isaiah 66:18)

Christians are called to reflect God's glory to the world, and today's verse encourages us that our witness will be successful. God declares that he will personally gather all nations to see his glory. In its immediate context, this verse may be a reference to God gathering those nations who are his enemies—those who had opposed his people Israel—to witness his glorious and gracious act of restoring his people to their homeland after 70 years in exile.

A larger context may also be considered, in view of Isaiah's previous predictions that "all flesh" would see the glory of God, as it would fill the whole earth "as the waters cover the sea." The book of Revelation speaks of men and women from every family, tribe, nation, and language worshipping before God's throne:

After this I looked, and there before me was a great multitude that no one could count, from every nation, tribe, people and language, standing before the throne and before the Lamb. They were wearing white robes and were holding palm branches in their hands. And they cried out in a loud voice: "Salvation belongs to our God, who sits on the throne, and to the Lamb." (Revelation 7:9–12)

This is a very powerful encouragement for us to carry on our efforts to win others for Jesus. God's purpose is our success, not our defeat.

Prayer: Lord, we praise you that, at this time of year especially, we can testify to our faith in your miraculous birth, sinless life, atoning death, and victorious resurrection. We pray that through this message of your glory revealed in Christ, you will draw all peoples to yourself. In Jesus' name. Amen.

Advent Reading Plan Day Eleven: John 11; Luke 2:36–40.

Thursday 13th December: *Abundant Glory*

> *For the earth will be filled with the knowledge of the Lord as the waters cover the sea. (Isaiah 11:9)*

Isaiah hoped for a future day when God's glory, in an inexpressibly abundant measure, would flood the world with the atmosphere of heaven. This major theme in Isaiah is inextricably linked with the hope of the coming Messiah. For Isaiah, only when Messiah rules the world will the glory of God fill the earth. Christ revealed God's glory through his miracles of compassion and healing; he further revealed God's glory through his death and resurrection; but his glory shall be fully and finally revealed when Jesus comes again.

Isaiah offers an amazing picture of that time:

> *The wolf will live with the lamb, the leopard will lie down with the goat, the calf and the lion and the yearling together; and a little child will lead them. The cow will feed with the bear, their young will lie down together, and the lion will eat straw like the ox. The infant will play near the cobra's den, the young child will put its hand into the viper's nest. They will neither harm nor destroy on all my holy mountain, for the earth will be filled with the knowledge of the Lord as the waters cover the sea. (Isaiah 11:6–9)*

To what extent these predictions are literal or symbolic is disputed. Yet Isaiah's vision clearly links Christ's coming with the restoration of creation, and, as the angels announced over the fields of Bethlehem, "peace on earth." Christ's work of bringing peace began the moment he was born, continued through his life, and will be completed when he comes "on the clouds of heaven in power and in great glory" (Matt 24:30).

> **Prayer:** Lord, your coming again in glory will mean the restoration of creation, and the dawning of your reign on earth as Prince of peace. Grant that as we await this day, we shall do all we can to promote "peace on earth." In Jesus' name. Amen.

Advent Reading Plan Day Twelve: John 12; Luke 2:41–52.

Friday 14th December: *Sharing the Glory of God*

> *In that day the Lord Almighty will be a glorious crown, a beautiful wreath for the remnant of his people. (Isaiah 28:5)*

The thought of God's children sharing His glory occurs repeatedly throughout Scripture. The Psalmist long ago considered the theme of sharing in God's likeness. He wrote:

> *As for me, I will see Your face in righteousness; I shall be satisfied when I awake in Your likeness. (Psalm 17:15 NKJV)*

The writers of the New Testament viewed glorification in terms of our being transformed into the likeness of the glorified Christ. Paul believed that contemplating God's glory transformed our hearts (2 Corinthians 3:18) and minds (Romans 12:2); but he also described the believer's future resurrection in terms of our bodies being fashioned in Christ's likeness:

> *who, by the power that enables him to bring everything under his control, will transform our lowly bodies so that they will be like his glorious body. (Philippians 3:21)*

Persecuted Christians were encouraged to look forward to sharing in the glory of God:

> *Now if we are children, then we are heirs—heirs of God and co-heirs with Christ, if indeed we share in his sufferings in order that we may also share in his glory. (Romans 8:17)*

The church will, in the future age, be seen to share God's glory:

> *And he ... and showed me the great city, the holy Jerusalem, descending out of heaven from God, having the glory of God. (Revelation 21:10–11 NKJV)*

The Lord God is a beautiful and glorious crown for His people!

> **Prayer:** God of glory, you have chosen us by your grace to be conformed to the image of your Son and share his eternal glory. Help us to live for your glory today. In Jesus' name. Amen.

Advent Reading Plan Day Thirteen: John 13; Luke 3:1–6.

Saturday 15th December: *The Coming King of Glory*

In my vision at night I looked, and there before me was one like a son of man, coming with the clouds of heaven. He approached the Ancient of Days and was led into his presence. He was given authority, glory and sovereign power; all nations and peoples of every language worshiped him. His dominion is an everlasting dominion that will not pass away, and his kingdom is one that will never be destroyed. (Daniel 7:13–14)

Jesus understood the prophet Daniel's vision of "one like a son of man" to be a reference to himself. Jesus was "the son of man," and when on trial for his life before the Sanhedrin, he announced, "From now on you will see the Son of Man sitting at the right hand of the Mighty One and coming on the clouds of heaven" (Matthew 26:64).

That glory is linked of course with his authority over all nations:

Then Jesus came to them and said, "All authority in heaven and on earth has been given to me." (Matthew 28:18)

Peter proclaimed on the day of Pentecost, and in the days following, that Jesus Christ "is Lord of all" (see Acts 2:36; 10:36). The reason his rule is over all people is that he died for all (Romans 14:9). The reason his rule is unending is that he can never die again:

For we know that since Christ was raised from the dead, he cannot die again; death no longer has mastery over him. (Romans 6:9)

It is this same eternal, deathless life which Christ promises to all who believe (John 3:16).

Prayer: Thine be the glory, risen conquering Son, endless is the victory, thou o'er death hast won. We thank you Lord that your victory over death has brought us everlasting life. We praise you that one day you will return in glory as king over all the earth. Hallelujah. Amen.

Advent Reading Plan Day Fourteen: John 14; Matt 1:1–17.

Week 3: God's Glory Revealed in Christ

Sunday 16th December: *We Have Seen His Glory*

> *The Word became flesh and made his dwelling among us. We have seen his glory, the glory of the one and only Son, who came from the Father, full of grace and truth. (John 1:14)*

As we enter the third week of Advent, Christmas is not far away, the season for celebrating our Lord's incarnation. In Christ, the Word made flesh, the writings of the prophets have been fulfilled, and God's glory has been revealed among us to a greater extent than ever before.

Although many understand the incarnation of Christ to be a "veiling" of God's glory, the New Testament writers saw it as the exact opposite. "We have seen his glory," writes John. In the Old Testament, Moses wore a veil to hide the glory of God—reflected on his face—from the people (2 Corinthians 3:13). But Paul assures us that in Christ "this veil is taken away" (2 Corinthians 3:16). Christ is:

> *the radiance of God's glory and the exact representation of his being, sustaining all things by his powerful word. (Hebrews 1:3)*

To see Jesus is to see God the Father (John 14:9). This is not a veiling, but an unveiling.

When God wanted the world to see his glory, he did not send a blinding light from heaven, our pour out shining flakes of gold—the symbol of this world's fading glory. That would be so far beneath him! Instead he wrapped up his glory in the flesh and blood of a baby, born in Bethlehem, who would declare himself to be God's gift to the world. Jesus is the full and complete revelation of the glory of God, the only one we need.

> **Prayer:** Dear God, we praise you that in Christ, your glory is not veiled, but revealed openly and perfectly, so that we might believe and receive eternal life. In Jesus' name. Amen.

Advent Reading Plan Day Fifteen: John 15; Matt 1:18–25.

Monday 17th December: *Manifesting His Glory*

> *What Jesus did here in Cana of Galilee was the first of the signs through which he revealed his glory; and his disciples believed in him. (John 2:11)*

Not only at his birth, but throughout his life, Jesus revealed the glory of God. Here, in the account of his first miracle — that of turning water into wine in Cana of Galilee — John records that Christ's intention was to reveal "his glory." John later clarifies that this glory is, "the glory I had with you [God] before the world began" (John 17:5).

Perhaps all the miracles Jesus performed, but especially those recorded in John's Gospel, may be thought of in the same way.

In New Testament thinking, the devil can make people ill, but only God can make them well. The world can leave someone broken, but only God can make them whole again. Sin can turn people bad, but only God can make them good. During his life and ministry, Jesus Christ demonstrated this saving, redeeming power of God:

> *God anointed Jesus of Nazareth with the Holy Spirit and power, and how he went around doing good and healing all who were under the power of the devil, because God was with him. (Acts 10:38)*

A single chapter in Luke's Gospel reveals how Jesus healed broken bodies (Luke 7:10), mended broken hearts (Luke 7:13–15), and transformed sinners into grateful and forgiven worshippers (Luke 7:36–50). This is still how Christ reveals God's glory today!

> **Prayer:** Lord, through your healing, comforting, and saving ministry, you still bring blessing and godly change to countless lives. Enable us at this season to be agents of your healing grace, reaching out to others in need. Strengthen those who will give their time this Christmas to help the sick, homeless, or lonely. In Jesus' name. Amen.

Advent Reading Plan Day Sixteen: John 16; Matt 2:1–12.

Tuesday 18th December: *The Glory to be Revealed in Us*

I consider that our present sufferings are not worth comparing with the glory that will be revealed in us. (Romans 8:18)

At a time when many will be enjoying the seasonal fun of Christmas events, today's verse focuses honestly on the reality of pain and suffering which are the unavoidable consequences of living in a fallen world.

The person who wrote this verse was Paul, who had experienced more than his fair share of suffering. Just a glance at his letters reveals how he had known pain, depression, violent persecution, hunger, homelessness, and imprisonment. Yet he considered even these hardships not worth comparing with the glory that shall be revealed in us.

The New Testament writers express the same hope in a variety of ways. When we see Jesus face to face we shall be changed into his likeness (1 John 3:2; Philippians 3:21). When the resurrection occurs, we shall exchange our mortality for immortality (1 Corinthians 15:53), and we shall be forever with the Lord (1 Thessalonians 4:17). When Jesus comes he will receive us to himself, that where he is we shall be also (John 14:3). All these ideas merge into one in today's simple verse. When we think of all that is ahead of us, our sufferings seem light by comparison. They cannot prevent us entering our eternal state, and when we have finally entered it, they will be forever forgotten in light of our glorious and eternal joy.

Prayer: Lord, we bring before you our pain and suffering. Grant us your help in our distress, and healing in our sickness. We praise you that whatever we experience, it is not worth comparing to the glorious future which you have planned for us. In Jesus' name. Amen.

Advent Reading Plan Day Seventeen: John 17; Matt 2:13–18.

Wednesday 19th December: *Riches in Glory*

And my God will meet all your needs according to the riches of his glory in Christ Jesus. (Philippians 4:19)

Here is the perfect promise for those who are struggling financially. Paul is writing to a small group of Christians who had sent him a gift to ease his suffering whilst he was imprisoned in Rome. Paul was so grateful for the expression of their love, but he was also sure they would not go without because of their sacrificial giving. He reminds them of Jesus' teaching that the God who feeds the sparrows will provide for their needs too.

Yet notice from where God provides our needs: his "riches in glory," or his "glorious riches." This provision extends far beyond our present experience and embraces all God's blessings for time and eternity. Paul used the same expression in Ephesians 3:16–19.

I pray that out of his glorious riches he may strengthen you with power through his Spirit in your inner being, so that Christ may dwell in your hearts through faith. And I pray that you, being rooted and established in love, may have power, together with all the Lord's holy people, to grasp how wide and long and high and deep is the love of Christ, and to know this love that surpasses knowledge—that you may be filled to the measure of all the fullness of God. (Ephesians 3:16–19)

Through Christ we can grow spiritually, and become established in faith, so that we can discover the glorious riches of the love of God.

Prayer: Lord, we thank you for providing all our needs, and for the power of your Holy Spirit who strengthens us so that Christ may dwell in our hearts by faith. We praise you for your love which is beyond our understanding. In Jesus' name. Amen

Advent Reading Plan Day Eighteen: John 18; Matt 2:19–23.

Thursday 20th December: *God Gave Him Glory*

Through him you believe in God, who raised him from the dead and glorified him, and so your faith and hope are in God. (1 Peter 1:21)

Some people are desperate to gain glory for themselves. Perhaps the modern trend of taking "selfies" and talking about ourselves on social media indicates that we all indulge in what the Bible calls "vain-glorying" from time to time! But pushing himself forward is exactly what Jesus did not do. The Bible describes his humility and tells us to follow his example.

Do nothing out of selfish ambition or vain conceit. Rather, in humility value others above yourselves, ... have the same mindset as Christ Jesus: Who, being in very nature God, did not consider equality with God something to be used to his own advantage; rather, he made himself nothing by taking the very nature of a servant, being made in human likeness. And being found in appearance as a man, he humbled himself by becoming obedient to death—even death on a cross! (Philippians 2:3–8)

The passage goes on to explain that although Christ did not exalt himself, God has highly exalted him:

Therefore God exalted him to the highest place and gave him the name that is above every name, that at the name of Jesus every knee should bow, in heaven and on earth and under the earth, and every tongue acknowledge that Jesus Christ is Lord, to the glory of God the Father. (Philippians 2:9–11)

The glory which Christ has can never be taken from him. Even his enemies shall be compelled one day to confess his Lordship.

Prayer: We thank you, O Lord, that whatever human authority may rule the land in which we live, and whatever burdens we may bear, ultimately the government of the whole world is, and ever shall be, on your shoulders. Amen.

Advent Reading Plan Day Nineteen: John 19; 1 John 1:1–5.

Friday 21st December: *To Him be Glory in the Church*

> *to him be glory in the church and in Christ Jesus throughout all generations, for ever and ever! Amen. (Ephesians 3:21)*

There are so many things which bring glory to God. For instance, we see his glory in the creation of the world of nature, and the vast universe. The psalmist wrote:

> *When I consider your heavens, the work of your fingers, the moon and the stars, which you have set in place, what is mankind that you are mindful of them, human beings that you care for them? (Psalm 8:3–4)*

Of course, as the above verse highlights, he is glorified in his Son Jesus Christ. Yet what is perhaps more surprising is that God is glorified in his church and will be so forever.

This may at first surprise us, because our many faults and failings could make us suppose that we hinder, rather than display the glory of God. But God is not glorified by human endeavours, but by his work of grace in human lives. Through Christ, God transforms sinners into saints. They are not perfect, but they are born again to share God's divine nature, and one day will inherit the perfection Christ has obtained for them. It is at that time God will receive tremendous praise for his glorious grace (Ephesians 1:6).

Even now, the existence of the church reveals God's love and grace for rebels and sinners—what a love, what a God, what glory!

> **Prayer:** Lord, we thank you for the great love you have bestowed on us, and praise you that because of your grace, we are part of your church, through which you shall be glorified forever. In Jesus' name. Amen.

Advent Reading Plan Day Twenty: John 20; 1 John 1:6–10.

Saturday 22nd December: *Coming in Clouds with Glory*

> *Then will appear the sign of the Son of Man in heaven. And then all the peoples of the earth will mourn when they see the Son of Man coming on the clouds of heaven, with power and great glory. (Matthew 24:30)*

As we prepare our hearts to celebrate Christ's first coming, so we prepare our heart in readiness for his second coming. The expectation of Christ's personal return to earth is still the blessed hope of his people (Titus 2:13). Yet many of the things Jesus says about his return concern his role as God-appointed judge of the wicked and unbelieving (e.g. Matthew 16:27; 25:31–46; Luke 9:26. See also 2 Thessalonians 1:7–8; Jude 1:14–15; Revelation 1:7).

In the verse above, Christ's return is an occasion for mourning among the unrepentant, who clearly see that they can no longer escape judgment. But for the believer in Christ, the time will also be one of unspeakable joy, when "the righteous will shine like the sun in the kingdom of their Father" (Matthew 13:43).

Christ comes in glory that he might reign in glory. In a passage which describes the blessings the Messianic reign, Isaiah announces:

> *He will judge between the nations and will settle disputes for many peoples. They will beat their swords into plowshares and their spears into pruning hooks. Nation will not take up sword against nation, nor will they train for war anymore. (Isaiah 2:4)*

Persecuted Christians around the world shall be delivered (2 Timothy 2:12) and justice granted to the martyrs (Revelation 6:10–11). Let us reaffirm again our faith in the personal coming of Christ as Prince of peace and King of kings to reign!

> **Prayer:** God my Saviour, as you have blessed my life with your strength and deliverance, help me to bless others by telling them how they too may know your salvation. In Jesus' name. Amen.

Advent Reading Plan Day Twenty-One: John 21; 1 John 2.

Week 4: To God be the Glory!

Sunday 23rd December: *Songs of Praise to God's Glory*

> *And behold, an angel of the Lord stood before them, and the glory of the Lord shone around them, and they were greatly afraid. ... "Glory to God in the highest, And on earth peace, goodwill toward men!" (Luke 2:9, 14 NKJV)*

The angels' song of praise over the hills of Bethlehem is still with us today; it is the theme of many carols being sung up and down the country at this time of year. A careful evaluation of Scripture may help to shed some light on what occasioned such an enduring hymn of praise.

Firstly, the angels had never seen the invisible God. He is "immortal, invisible," even to their eyes. Although God is Spirit, and angels are also spirits, clearly they are of a different order—angels are created spirits, whereas God is uncreated—and hence he remains invisible to them. In a stable in Bethlehem, for the first time, God was manifest in the flesh, and so at last was "seen by angels" (1 Timothy 3:16). That is why the occasion was so awesome to them!

Secondly, God's plan of salvation, which was being unveiled by the birth of Christ, was a plan of such scope and scale that it was something even the angels longed to investigate (1 Peter 1:12). The Son of God became flesh and blood that he might redeem humanity—and as a result the redeemed have a song which angels can never sing.

No wonder the angels were so interested! It's simply amazing that God in his love should give his only Son, and through him offer pardon and peace to a rebellious world!

> **Prayer:** Lord, we join with the angels in praising you this Christmas season. We are amazed that the invisible God became flesh that he might suffer and die for our sins, bringing us peace with God, and peace with all people. Hallelujah! Amen.

Advent Reading Plan Day Twenty-Two: 1 John 3; Galatians 4:1–7.

Christmas Eve: *The Radiance of God's Glory*

> *The Son is the radiance of God's glory and the exact representation of his being, sustaining all things by his powerful word. After he had provided purification for sins, he sat down at the right hand of the Majesty in heaven. (Hebrews 1:3)*

It's Christmas Eve—time for us to look again at the baby of Bethlehem. He is worth a long and careful look, for as the writer to the Hebrews says, he expresses God's nature and glory in a unique and powerful way. The New Testament writers comprehend Jesus as God. Even as he lay in the animal's feeding trough, he was the Word made flesh. Even as the donkey brushed against his makeshift crib, he remained the one who "sustains all things by the word of his power," (Hebrews 1:3) keeping all the countless stars in place—stars he had named!

Some theologians speak of Jesus as laying aside his glory to be born into this world. The New Testament presents quite a different picture, that of Christ being the perfect manifestation of God's glory (see 2 Corinthians 4:4; Colossians 1:15–16).

Others speak of Christ emptying himself to become human, whereas the New Testament speaks not of emptiness but the "fulness of the godhead" dwelling in him "in bodily form" (Colossians 2:9). Jesus Christ came to reveal God's glory, a glory which is "full of grace and truth" (John 1:14).

The radiance of God's glory reaches out to you and me, inviting us in, to love the one who first loved us, worship the one who was born to redeem us, and praise the name of the one who died, so that the costly rescue mission he began at Bethlehem could be accomplished.

> **Prayer:** Lord, we praise you for the glory of Christmas—that God is with us and will never leave us. We praise you, for you so loved us, that gave up your heavenly home, shedding your blood on the cross to save us. It is this love, more than anything else, that reveals the fulness of God's glory to us. Amen.

Advent Reading Plan Day Twenty-Three: 1 John 4; 1 Tim 3:16.

Christmas Day: *The Glory of Christ Within*

> *To them God has chosen to make known among the Gentiles the glorious riches of this mystery, which is Christ in you, the hope of glory. ... When Christ, who is your life, appears, then you also will appear with him in glory. (Colossians 1:27; 3:4)*

The most wonderful revelation of Christmas is not the glory of Christ in the manger, nor of Christ on the cross, nor even empty tomb. The most "glorious mystery" of our faith is "Christ in you, the hope of glory." It is that Christ the Lord of glory is a present reality in our daily lives, even this Christmas Day.

In Colossians, Paul goes further, saying that the glory of Christ within us is also the "hope of glory," which is to say, it is the promise of glory yet to come. He immediately goes on to explain that when Christ appears (his Parousia, or second coming) we will appear with him in glory. This thought equates very closely with that expressed in 1 Thessalonians 4:13–18 (opposite page), that those who are Christ's, both the living and the dead, shall be with him at his coming, and there will be a great reunion.

I remember our vicar once saying that every Christmas Day, he left a place at the dinner table for his dad, who died several years ago. Each Christmas, a drink is poured, and dad is remembered and missed. I can fully relate to this, and I have no doubt that the reader also knows the pain of missing loved ones at this time of year. Yet the hope we have in Jesus includes the hope that "God will bring with Jesus those who are asleep in him." It's another Christmas without them, but it is another Christmas closer to them—closer to Christ's glorious appearing, and our joyous reunion.

> **Prayer:** Lord, on this holy day, comfort and strengthen all who grieve, and all those who for any reason feel the pain of an absent loved one. We praise you that for all who are in Christ, a day is coming when no one shall ever part us from you or each other. In Jesus' name. Amen.

Advent Reading Plan Twenty-Four: 1 John 5.

Believers Who Have Died

Brothers and sisters, we do not want you to be uninformed about those who sleep in death, so that you do not grieve like the rest of mankind, who have no hope. For we believe that Jesus died and rose again, and so we believe that God will bring with Jesus those who have fallen asleep in him. According to the Lord's word, we tell you that we who are still alive, who are left until the coming of the Lord, will certainly not precede those who have fallen asleep. For the Lord himself will come down from heaven, with a loud command, with the voice of the archangel and with the trumpet call of God, and the dead in Christ will rise first. After that, we who are still alive and are left will be caught up together with them in the clouds to meet the Lord in the air. And so we will be with the Lord forever. Therefore encourage one another with these words.

(1 Thessalonians 4:13–18)